EASTER FUN

Kingfisher

NEW YORK

KINGFISHER
Larousse Kingfisher Chambers Inc.
95 Madison Avenue
New York, New York 10016

2 4 6 8 10 9 7 5 3 1
Copyright © Larousse plc 1996

LIBRARY OF CONGRESS CATALOGING-IN-PUBLICATION DATA
Robins, Deri.
Easter fun / written by Deri Robins; illustrated by Maggie
Downer.—1st American ed.
p. cm.
Summary: Includes instructions for making baskets, pompom animals,
a card mobile, colorful eggs, paper flowers, Easter breads, and
other items to celebrate this holiday.
1. Easter decorations—Juvenile literature. 2. Handicraft-—
Juvenile literature. 3. Easter cookery—Juvenile literature.
[1. Easter decorations. 2. Handicraft.] I. Downer, Maggie, ill.
II. Title.
TT900.E2R63   1996
745.694-1—dc20   95-37308 CIP AC

ISBN 1-85697-667-X

Printed in Spain

CONTENTS

EASTER TIME

The long, dark winter months are over—spring has finally arrived! There are signs of new life everywhere—leaves and buds cover the trees, birds start building their nests, and each day is a little longer than the one before it.

People have celebrated the arrival of spring for thousands of years. Long ago, winter meant great hardship for most people. Their homes were dark and cold, and food supplies often ran dangerously low. When spring came around again and new crops began to grow, it was a time of great rejoicing. The people gave thanks to the goddess Eostre, from whose name we get our word "Easter."

Today, many religious festivals are held in the spring. There's Easter itself, of course—one of the most important dates in the Christian calendar. The Jewish Passover and the Indian festival of Holi are also held at this time. For everyone, it's a time for fun, celebration, and new beginnings.

There's plenty to do, so let's get going!

4

SEEDS FOR SPRING

Everywhere you look, trees and flowers are putting out shoots and leaves. You can make a springtime garden on your own windowsill—all you need are some seeds!

You will need

Apples, oranges, lemons, and grapes (All have seeds inside from which new plants can grow. Use them to grow pretty houseplants—they may even bear fruit one day, but don't count on it!)

1 Fill a small seed tray with potting soil (or use a clean plastic container). Bury some seeds in the soil, about 3" apart.

3 When the shoots have about four leaves, plant them in separate flower-pots.

You can also try planting garlic cloves, or the top of an onion.

2 Water the soil, and put the tray in a warm, light place until shoots start to appear.

orange plant

onion plant

PAPER FLOWERS

If you can't wait for the springtime flowers to come out, you can make a bright bouquet of paper blooms—they'll come in handy for decorating your Easter bonnet, and would also make a great gift for Mother's Day!

You will need

crepe paper in different colors (including green) green paper, thin cardboard thin garden wire, or some thin sticks. cotton balls scissors, glue

1 Ask an adult to cut a piece of wire about 10" long (or use a thin stick). Tape a cotton ball to one end of the wire or stick.

2 Cut a small square of crepe paper and tie over the cotton ball.

3 Cut a long strip of the same paper, about 2½" wide. Fold it over about eight times to make a zigzag.

4 Draw one of these petal shapes onto the strip of paper and cut out to make eight petals.

5 Glue each petal just below the cotton ball wad, overlapping them slightly.

6 Cut a long, thin strip of green crepe paper. Glue one end around the top of the stem, wind tightly down like a bandage, and glue the other end to the bottom.

7 Cut more leaves out of cardboard, and glue these along the stem. When dry, gently pull back the edges of the petals.

This daffodil has a center made of paper, which is glued in separately.

Try cutting the petals into tiny strips to make a carnation.

CARDS FOR EASTER

Bunnies, chicks, and spring flowers all make good subjects for Easter cards—take your pick! The window box would also make a great Mother's Day card....

You will need

thin cardboard (15"x6")
scissors, glue
white tissue paper
scraps of fabric
colored construction
paper

WINDOW BOX

1 Fold the cardboard into thirds. Cut a window out of *a*. Fold over, draw an identical window onto *b*, and cut this out.

2 Glue tissue paper over window *b*. Stick a piece of fabric down on top, to make a shade. Then glue *a* on top of *b*.

3 Cut a window box out of cardboard and glue to the front. Cut flowers, leaves, and stems out of construction paper, and glue these on, too.

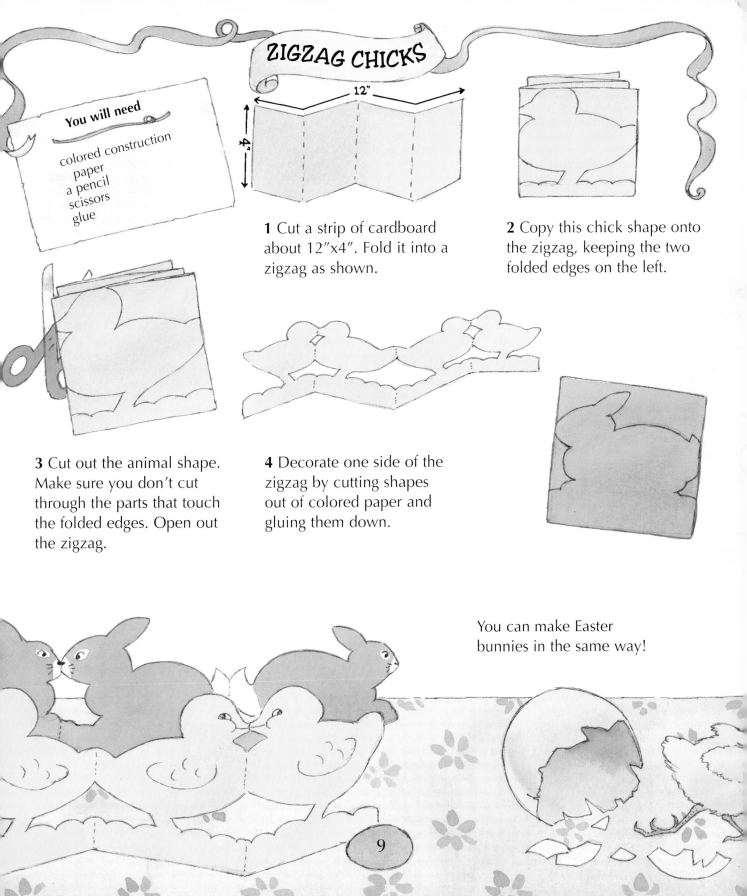

ZIGZAG CHICKS

12"

4"

1 Cut a strip of cardboard about 12"x4". Fold it into a zigzag as shown.

2 Copy this chick shape onto the zigzag, keeping the two folded edges on the left.

3 Cut out the animal shape. Make sure you don't cut through the parts that touch the folded edges. Open out the zigzag.

4 Decorate one side of the zigzag by cutting shapes out of colored paper and gluing them down.

You can make Easter bunnies in the same way!

ALL ABOUT EGGS

Easter wouldn't be Easter without eggs! All around the world, children look forward to a visit from the Easter Bunny, who hides eggs around the house and yard. There are all kinds of eggy games to play, too—like tossing hard-boiled eggs in the air, racing with an egg on a spoon, or rolling them down a hill! Decorating eggs is another important tradition. Here are some ideas to try.

BLOWING EGGS

Blown eggs are more fragile than hard-boiled ones, but you can pack them away after Easter and keep them for many years to come.

Make a hole in each end with a pin. Then carefully make the holes bigger with a nail (the bottom hole needs to be about $1/2''$ across, but the top can be much smaller).

Hold the egg over a bowl, and blow out the yolk and white. Keep these for cooking. The egg is easier to decorate if you push a knitting needle through the holes. Hold in place with modeling clay.

COLORED EGGS

You will need

eggs (white ones are best for dyeing)
food for making dyes—try onion skins, raw beets, turmeric, spinach leaves, or grapes.
vinegar

1 Half fill a small saucepan with water. Add drops of vinegar and one of the following: onion or spinach leaves, half a beet, a heaped teaspoon of turmeric, or a few grapes.

2 Ask an adult to boil the water for 30 minutes. Dip eggs in the water when it has cooled, and leave until they change color. Leave to dry.

PRETTY PATTERNS

You will need

masking tape
food dyes or paint

1 Cut the masking tape into shapes—like the petals of a flower. Press gently but firmly onto the egg.

2 Dye the egg or paint all over the shell. When dry, peel off the masking tape to see the pattern.

EGGCELLENT IDEAS

You can simply paint the eggs freehand or glue on paper flowers, lace, and braid. Try turning the eggs into faces or animals. Cloth, paper, and yarn make hair, tails, and ears.

1 Cut a potato in half and cut a simple pattern on the flat surface. Dip into paint and press *gently* onto the surface of the egg, to make a repeating pattern.

2 Wash your egg out carefully, and ask an adult to help you fill it with melted chocolate or Jell-O. Put it in the fridge to set—and give someone a surprise at breakfast!

PAPIER MÂCHÉ EGGS

You will need

an oval balloon
newspaper
2 cups flour
4 cups water
paints
varnish

1 Ask an adult to heat the water and flour in a pan until the mixture looks like cake batter. Let it cool.

2 Tear the paper into small strips. Ask an adult to blow up the balloon.

3 Dip the paper strips into the paste, and smooth them onto the balloon. Make at least seven layers.

4 When it's dry paint it to look like a big Easter egg, or cut it in half into two Mardi Gras masks!

Finish off with a coat of varnish.

EASTER TREE

Show off your eggs and other decorations by hanging them on an Easter "tree"! About four weeks before Easter, look for a large branch covered with buds. If you put this in water and keep it in a warm room, the branch should be covered with tiny leaves by Easter Sunday.

HANG YOUR EGGS

1 Cut some thread into 5" lengths. Snap some used wooden matchsticks in half, then tie one end of a piece of thread to a matchstick half.

2 Carefully poke the matchstick through the top hole in the egg. Pull the thread so that the matchstick lies across the hole inside the egg.

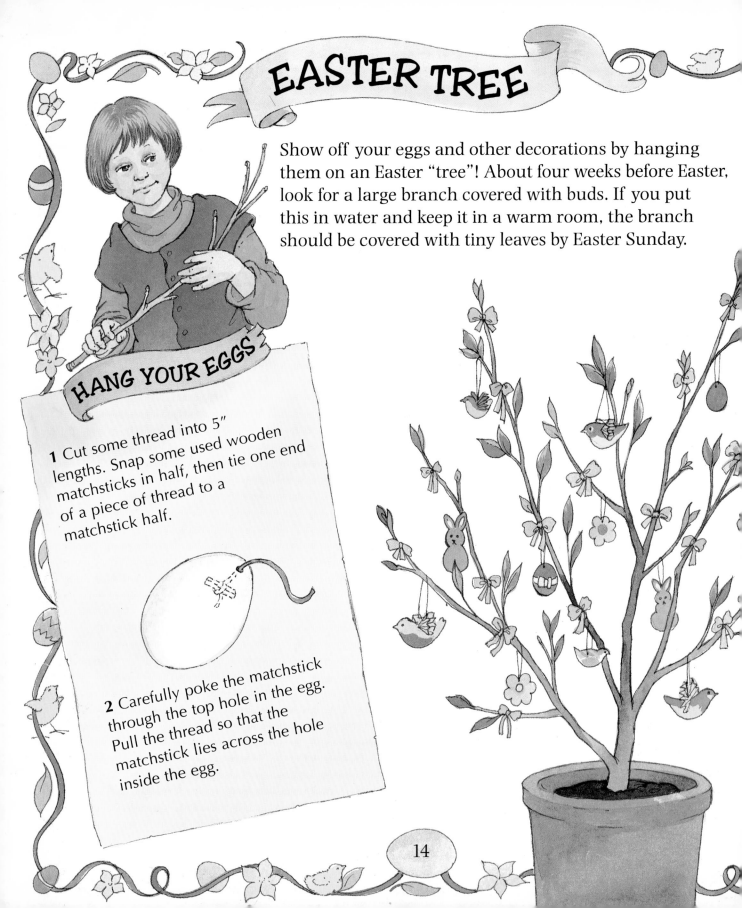

14

PAPER BIRDS

You will need

thin colored cardboard
colored tissue paper
tracing paper, pencil
scissors
a needle and thread

1 Trace the bird's body (above) onto the cardboard, and cut it out. Cut out the slit in the middle.

2 Cut a rectangle out of tissue paper, measuring 5"x3". Fold it into a zigzag, as shown above.

3 Push the folded tissue paper through the bird's body. Fan out the wings.

4 Thread a needle, and push it through the top of the wings. Knot to hold in place.

CLAY SHAPES

You will need

self-hardening clay
poster paints
varnish

1 Cover a board with plastic wrap, then roll out the clay to about 1/4" thick.

2 Cut out Easter shapes with a blunt knife. Make a small hole in the top of each shape.

3 Let them dry for a day or two. Paint both sides, coat with varnish, and hang on the tree.

MAKE A MOBILE

This chirpy nest of chicks makes a perfect Easter decoration—you could also make an extra one, and give it to someone as a special present.

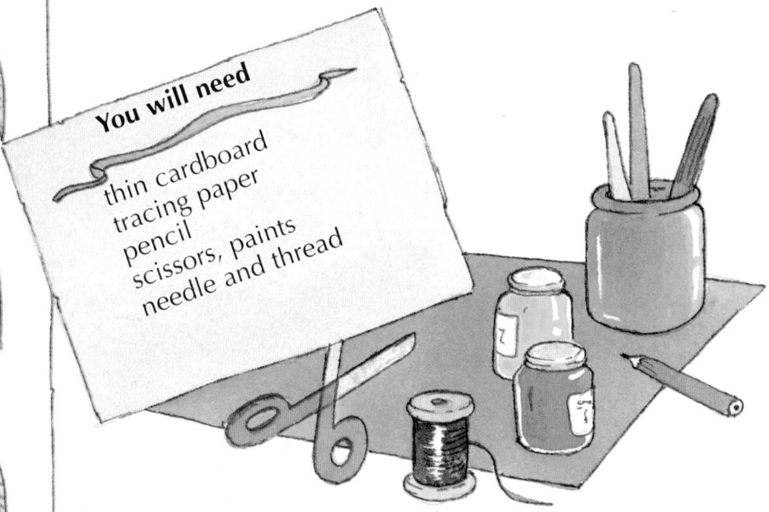

You will need

thin cardboard
tracing paper
pencil
scissors, paints
needle and thread

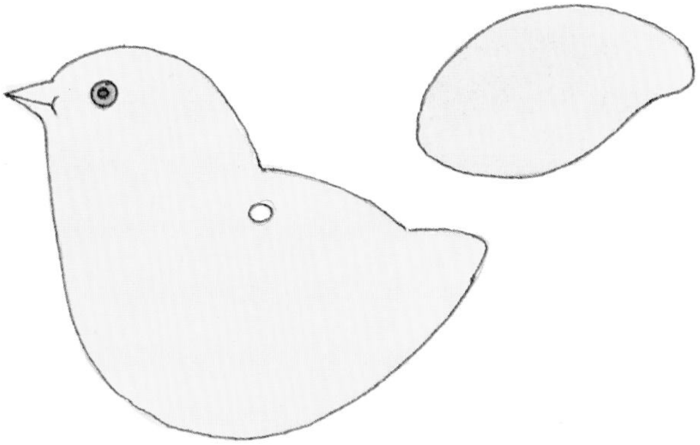

1 Trace the tree canopy twice onto cardboard, and cut out. Paint both sides green, and leave to dry.

2 Cut out four chicks and eight wings. Paint both sides of the chicks, and one side of the wings.

3 Trace and cut out the nest full of broken eggs and paint this, too. Leave to dry.

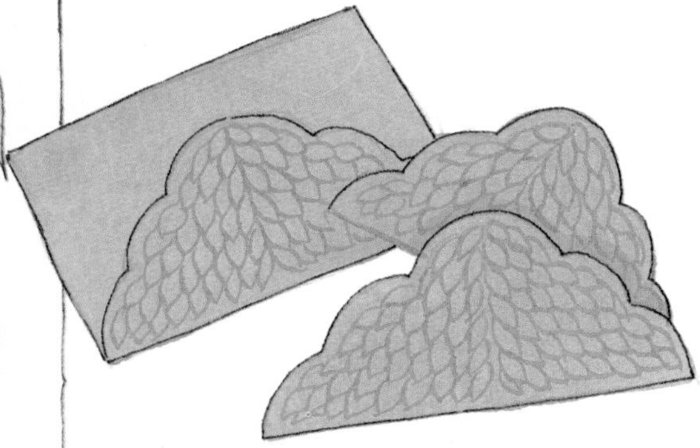

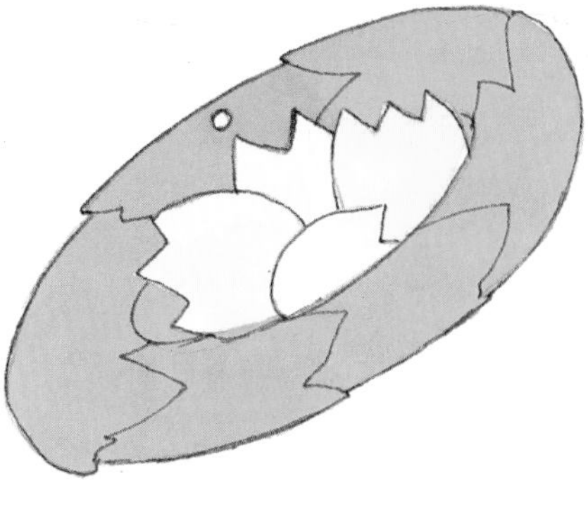

4 Cut a slit at the top of one of the canopy pieces, and at the bottom of the other. Slot them together.

5 Put a little glue on the unpainted side of the wings and stick them to the chicks' bodies.

6 Use the needle and thread to attach the pieces to each other, as shown below.

BOXES AND BASKETS

Jelly beans and Easter eggs look even more exciting when they come in a special basket—here's how to make your own out of paper.

4½"   2½"   3½"

BUNNY BASKET

All you need is some colored construction paper a pencil and ruler scissors and glue

1 Copy the above pattern onto the paper, to the measurements given. Cut out and fold up to make a box. Then glue the flaps inside the box as shown below.

2 Fold a piece of paper in half and then draw a long-eared bunny's head on the front. Cut out the shape, but *don't* cut the top of the ears.

3 Glue the bunny to the basket— the ears will make the handles. Line with crumpled tissue paper.

18

WOVEN BASKETS

Again, all you will need is some colored construction paper
a pencil and ruler
scissors, and
glue

½" border

1 Copy this pattern onto the paper, to the given measurements. Cut it out.

3½"

3½"

3½"

2 Cut six slits on each side. Leave a border about ½" wide along the top of each side.

3 Cut six strips of colored paper, each about ½"x 12" long.

4 Fold up the sides of the box. Weave a strip through all four sides, as shown. Glue the ends down.

5 Continue weaving up to the top. Go *over* the slits where the strip below went *under*. Glue on a handle and add decorations.

19

FUNNY BUNNY

Cute fluffy bunnies (not to mention chicks and lambs) can easily be made from yarn pompoms!

1 Wind some yarn around two rings cut out of cardboard (3" across).

2 Keep winding pieces of yarn around the rings, until the hole in the middle is nearly full.

3 Ask an adult to push the point of the scissors between the rings, and cut the yarn.

4 Ease the rings slightly apart, and tie a piece of yarn firmly around the middle. Pull off the rings.

5 Make another pompom, using rings about 1½" wide. Tie the pompoms together with the loose pieces of yarn.

▲ A brown or gray Easter bunny can have a pair of floppy felt ears and a felt nose. Sew on small beads or buttons for eyes.

▶ Sew or glue a diamond of felt to this chick's head. To make legs, just wind a pipe cleaner around the middle of the body before tying on the head.

◀ Make a lamb from white pompoms, add floppy black felt ears and a tail, and two pipe cleaners for legs.

Think up some more baby animals to add to your spring collection!

EASTER BREAD

Jelly beans and chocolate eggs are a fairly modern idea, but the tradition of baking special buns and breads for Easter goes back thousands of years. Here are two delicious recipes to try at home.

PRETZELS

You will need

a package of yeast
1½ cups warm water
1 teaspoon salt
4 cups sifted flour
1 tablespoon sugar
1 egg
coarse salt

Preheat the oven to 425°F

1 Empty the package of yeast into a big bowl, and pour in the water. Leave for about five minutes.

2 Add the salt, sugar, and flour to the yeast and stir well. Form the dough into a ball with your hands.

3 Knead the dough for about five minutes until it's smooth and stretchy.

4 Divide dough into 24 balls and roll into thin sticks. Twist sticks as shown.

5 Grease some large cookie sheets and put the pretzels on them. Space them out well.

6 Brush pretzels with a little egg and sprinkle with salt. Ask an adult to put them in the oven for 20 minutes.

22

You will need

¹/₂ package yeast
3 cups sifted flour
pinch of salt
1 tablespoon vegetable
    oil
1 cup warm water
1 egg

Preheat the oven to 450°F

EASTER ROLLS

1 Empty the yeast, salt, and flour into a large bowl and pour in the oil and water.

2 Mix into a dough and knead for five minutes. Divide the mixture into tangerine-sized balls.

3 Form the balls into fun Easter shapes, then put in a warm place for half an hour. Your rolls should double in size.

4 You can now decorate your rolls—raisins, nuts, poppy seeds, and sesame seeds are good for this.

5 Ask an adult to bake the rolls for about 20 minutes. Cool, but eat them while they're still warm!

23

SWEET TREATS

Here are some delicious treats to finish off the Easter feast!

CANDY NESTS

You will need

¹/₂ cup margarine
¹/₄ cup dark brown sugar
2 tablespoons corn syrup
2 tablespoons cocoa powder
1¹/₂ cups shredded wheat cereal

1 Put the margarine, sugar, and syrup in a pan. Ask an adult to heat it gently until melted.

2 Stir in the cocoa. Crush the cereal, and stir this in too. Leave to cool slightly.

3 Shape into small nests. Lightly grease a baking sheet, and put the nests on the sheet. Leave in a cool place to set.

You can fill your nests with jelly beans and chocolate eggs—or try some of the ideas shown opposite . . . .

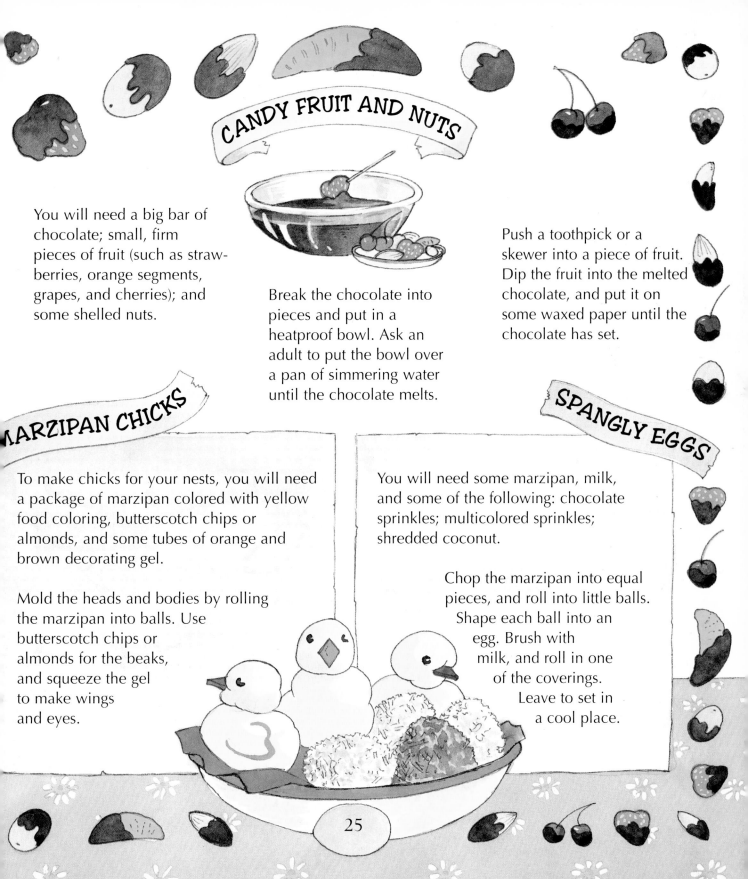

CANDY FRUIT AND NUTS

You will need a big bar of chocolate; small, firm pieces of fruit (such as strawberries, orange segments, grapes, and cherries); and some shelled nuts.

Break the chocolate into pieces and put in a heatproof bowl. Ask an adult to put the bowl over a pan of simmering water until the chocolate melts.

Push a toothpick or a skewer into a piece of fruit. Dip the fruit into the melted chocolate, and put it on some waxed paper until the chocolate has set.

MARZIPAN CHICKS

To make chicks for your nests, you will need a package of marzipan colored with yellow food coloring, butterscotch chips or almonds, and some tubes of orange and brown decorating gel.

Mold the heads and bodies by rolling the marzipan into balls. Use butterscotch chips or almonds for the beaks, and squeeze the gel to make wings and eyes.

SPANGLY EGGS

You will need some marzipan, milk, and some of the following: chocolate sprinkles; multicolored sprinkles; shredded coconut.

Chop the marzipan into equal pieces, and roll into little balls. Shape each ball into an egg. Brush with milk, and roll in one of the coverings. Leave to set in a cool place.

25

EASTER BONNETS

To make a hat or bonnet for the Easter parade, you'll need thin cardboard, colored construction paper, paints, glue, and scissors. For the bonnet, you'll also need paper flowers (pages 6-7).

FLOWER BONNETS

1 Cut a circle out of cardboard, following this pattern. Cut it out and paint it to look like a straw bonnet.

2 Draw a little circle in the center and draw four lines inside it. Cut along these lines. Bend up as shown.

3 Make lots of paper flowers (see page 6-7), keeping the stems short.

4 Glue the flowers all around the brim of the hat, overlapping them to hide the stems.

22"

1 Cut a strip of paper, about 10"x22", and draw a line down the middle.

2 Cut slits as far as this line all along one of the long edges.

3 Curl the strip around your head to check the fit, then glue or staple the ends in place.

4 Take two opposite strips, and glue them together. Do the same thing with the rest of the strips.

EXTRA IDEAS

Sew crepe paper petals to a long, thin scarf, and tie the ends under your chin!

A simple strip of cardboard with long ears makes a bunny hat!

5 Draw around the hat onto cardboard. Draw a slightly bigger circle around it. Cut this rim out. Glue to the hat as shown.

6 Paint a pattern onto the hat, or glue on shapes cut out of colored paper.

If there's a light breeze blowing, why not make and fly this special Easter kite?

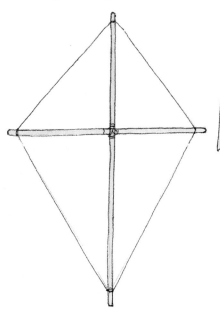

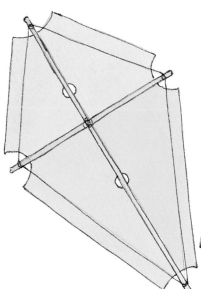

1 Tie the sticks into a cross with string. Then tie string from corner to corner as shown.

2 Put the kite frame onto the plastic and draw around it. Draw a border about 2" wide. Cut two holes, as shown, and cut half-circles at each corner.

3 Strengthen the holes and corners with tape. Then cut your Easter design out of paper and glue to one side.

4 Lay the frame on the other side and tape the sides firmly over the string.

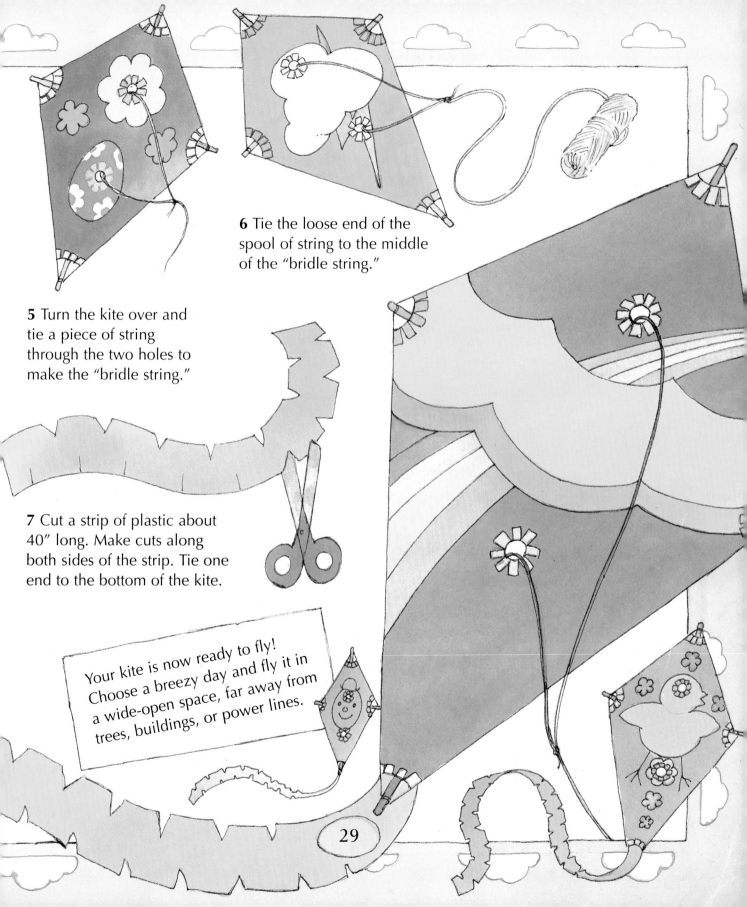

6 Tie the loose end of the spool of string to the middle of the "bridle string."

5 Turn the kite over and tie a piece of string through the two holes to make the "bridle string."

7 Cut a strip of plastic about 40" long. Make cuts along both sides of the strip. Tie one end to the bottom of the kite.

Your kite is now ready to fly! Choose a breezy day and fly it in a wide-open space, far away from trees, buildings, or power lines.

29

EASTER TRAILS

Here are three different kinds of treasure trails to leave for your family and friends on Easter Sunday—it's up to you what kind of prize they find at the end of it!

TREASURE HUNT

Make a separate trail for each friend, and see who gets to their prize first!

Write out about twelve clues on separate pieces of paper. Each clue will direct your friends to the next one. The final clue tells them where to find their Easter treat!

Don't make it too easy! If the next clue is in an umbrella, you could write "I only go up when something else comes down." Or use a simple code—for example, write all the words and letters backward!

look inside
the bucket

PICTURE TRAILS

Divide your friends into teams—each team needs at least two players.

Hide a separate trail for each team. This time the instructions can be quite straightforward. Give one player in each team the first clue, a pad of paper, and a pencil.

The player *draws* the clue on the paper —no words allowed! The rest of the team must look at the drawing to find the next clue. Whoever finds the clue does the next drawing, and so on.

Although each team should be following a separate trail, the final clue should be the same for all teams. The prize goes to the team that was quickest on the draw!

TRACKER TRAIL

Try leaving a secret trail with sticks and stones—work out the signals with a friend so that you both understand it! Here are a few ideas to start you off—try making up some of your own.

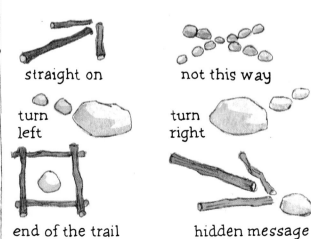

straight on   not this way

turn
left   turn
right

end of the trail   hidden message

31

SPRING CELEBRATIONS

Easter is only one of many springtime festivals that are celebrated around the world. How many others do you know?

Passover is a celebration of freedom. It's the time when Jewish people celebrate the escape of the Israelites from slavery in Egypt, many hundreds of years ago. It is usually celebrated by a special family meal called a Seder.

Purim takes place in February or March. It celebrates the story of Queen Esther, who saved the lives of all the Jews living in Persia (now called Iran). To celebrate this festival, Jewish people in many places have carnivals with big processions—it's a good excuse for both adults and children to put on costumes and dance in the streets!

Mother's Day in the U.S.A. is held on the second Sunday in May. This is the time we thank our mothers for all they do for us during the year, by giving them cards and presents—and maybe some help with the household chores!

April first is a time for tricks and practical jokes. In some parts of the world, you have to play the trick before noon, or the joke's on you!

Holi is an important springtime festival for Hindu people. It's a great time for feasting and merriment—including the custom of throwing colored powder over friends and passersby!